IMMANUEL IN THE Valley

When Bad Things Happen to Good People

BY KEITH A. BROWN SR.

Published by One Journey Publishing

Dedication

To my beautiful family.
You've been such a blessing to me.
I love you all!

Table of Contents

Table of Contents Con'd

When Bad Things Happen to Good People

The Illusion of Good

Let me start by saying no one is good but Jesus. As much as I would love to be called good, I know that I am just one bad decision away from sin. When I was growing up, people may have looked at me as kind of a goodie-two-shoes, because I didn't join the crowd on most things that were going on. For instance, If a bunch of us went into a store I didn't steal anything. If we were in a group around adults, I didn't use profanity. I didn't smoke, I wasn't a drinker, I respected women, I respected my elders. Put it this way, if I was in a group of people, I would quicker choose the right thing to do before the wrong. That doesn't mean that I never made mistakes.

When I was old enough to go to the clubs–because we all go through stages of growing up–I would see the same thing over and over again–sin. And what I found is that I was willfully participating in something that I would feel horrible about afterward. Oh, I forgot to mention that I have a huge conscience. People would be in there smoking, drinking, dancing provocatively, and I participated without my arm being twisted. Some, believe it or not, were in there forgetting their vows to their spouses. Not passing judgment because we all have a place where the Lord finds us and calls us out from. But yes, that was not my scene.

One night, I did wonder to myself why I kept coming to a place where the surroundings and the people were not my jam. This lifestyle went against everything I claimed to be as a Christian man. Just trying to fit in, I suppose–like forcing a square peg into a round hole. I thought I was a "good" person, but my actions would beg to differ. My flesh and my spirit were at war, and transparently, my flesh was winning most battles.

But that's just it. We can't run or hide from sin because we were born into it. No fault of our own, but because of the "Fall of Man" in the time of Adam and Eve. Jesus is the only one wrapped in flesh that could ever be called good. There are two things that come with that. One, He never said that we wouldn't suffer bad things. Two, if Jesus is the only one wrapped in flesh who could be called good–look at how much He suffered for us. Look at the bad things that happened to such a good man. This man that would lay down His life for a sinner like me.

No one is good but Jesus.

CHAPTER 1

I Desire to be Good

I considered myself to be a good person. I came from a family that loved me unconditionally, and a mom and dad that raised me with strong morals and values. In fact, our family is close-knit–full of love and a strong sense of right and wrong. This is a family that would give you the shirt from their backs. A loving and compassionate, God-fearing people. I thank God for the support system that I have in my family which has allowed me to walk into who God has called me to be with confidence.

I always wanted to be married because I was more of a one-woman type of man. Now, don't get me wrong, I had to grow up as well. Yes, I've had my fair share of fornicating–not proud of it but it was what it was. But when I got married, I knew for sure I would be happy forever, because after all, what woman doesn't want a man that's madly in love with them, right? Well, that didn't happen right away, but I'll tell you about that later.

Having been baptized at a very early age, I thought I knew God very well but had no idea that our relationship would grow so much as I got older. That being said, there was a time when I used profanity heavily and another where I didn't use it at all. While on my heavy use of it, I was still believing that I was representing God the right way even with a mouth I wouldn't kiss my own mother with. Somehow, all my friends still knew that I was a Christian and that Jesus meant the world to me. Only God can shine His light through a wretched man.

The Blunt

When I was about 19 years old, I smoked weed for the first time simply because my mother had accused me of being on drugs. She didn't actually accuse me, but more like, just asked the question. To be honest, she had every right to ask. See what had happened was... I was supposed to pick my beautiful mother up from work one day and I totally forgot. That doesn't sound like too much of a big deal, right? Well, there was something else that I had forgotten just the day prior, but I forgot what that was–Oh yeah! I was supposed to pick her up then too. So, when I forgot to pick my mom up from work two days in a row, she was upset and naturally asked me if I was on drugs. I said, "No Ma, it's me. I just forgot and I'm sorry."

I was really offended though, because it was me, but at that point in my life I think even I was unsure of what I could do that was outside of my norm. My mother had never had a problem from me. In fact, I was somewhat of a Momma's boy but not the way you think. My momma loved her son, and everyone knew it. I was the baby boy up until my baby brother. More to come on the beloved subject of him. But the fact that she even had to ask that question really offended me. And it was my fault. Petty.

The next night I was out with my brother. We had just gotten off work from a recycling plant. We were as dirty as two pigs freshly rolled in mud, but I made a quick stop to take him home. At this time, he lived in the northwest section of Washington, DC in an apartment building on a specific corner. The streets were still glistening from the early rain. I was diggin' one of the girls in the building, but she was not feelin' your boy!

Anyway, that girl's sister is the one that got me caught up.

We were standing in the alley in the back of the apartment building. It was her, her friend (another girl), and me. We were just standing there talking and laughing when all of a sudden, she pulled out this fat blunt and lit it up. Just think, "eyeballs looking to the right" emoji! The orangey lit ring–around the ashed tip of the blunt–in the dark alley looked like a beacon of light, or a location sensor for anyone who enjoyed getting high. The smoke smelled like a very specific black and white creature that lives in the wild, who every now and then, finds its way into the city.

She started smoking and then she passes it to the other girl. When the girl passed the smoke, I skipped it because I said, "I've never done this before." Then I got hit with the oldest trick in the book. You know the one question that is the foundation of all peer pressure? The young lady who lit the blunt said to me, "You scared?" In which I replied, "No! Gimmie that thing!"

In my mind I was replaying how my mom "accused" me of being on drugs and how it offended me. I thought to myself, "Well, if she already accused me, I may as well go for it." Being totally led by the flesh, pride spoke before wisdom. I proceeded to smoke that smoke so good that the girl asked in astonishment, "I thought you said you never smoked before?" "I haven't," I said. "But you're smoking like you're a pro!" What I didn't tell her is that when I was young, I saw my dad smoke weed for years, and he was a pro. I was just imitating him. What affects did his actions–when I was small–have on me psychologically that I didn't know about? Was I going to be another link in an unbroken chain of drug addiction or was I going to be able to rise above historical demons that didn't belong to me?

My Father's Redemption

My dad is an awesome man. Very strong minded, full of morals and values, loves to laugh, loves his family, and loves God. A real genuine type of person who calls a spade a spade. His favorite sport when I was growing up was basketball–I'm more than sure that's where I get it from. He battled with drug addiction in his early years, but somehow the Lord always brought him home every night. This is a true testament to Immanuel being with us in our valleys. Even in the lowest and darkest of places, He won't leave you.

He tells the story of one night being out with his friends free-basing cocaine, the TV was on and there was a Televangelist on saying, "Look at you, you're backsliding! Out there free-basing cocaine!" At that time one of my dad's friends said, "Look RG," (that's short for Robert Gene), "He's talking to you." My dad said, "Yeah, I believe he is. Y'all don't call me anymore for this $#@%!" That night when he got home, he fell to his knees and asked God to deliver him completely from his addiction. The way he described the deliverance was as if someone pulled out something from the inside of him. Just like that he was delivered and set free from drugs. There was no 12-step program or cold turkey sweats. He was fully delivered from his addiction when he got home and gave it to the Lord.

I had only smoked three times in my entire life, and it was all before the age of twenty-one. The other two times that I smoked where solely based on who I was hanging with at the time. I made a conscious effort to stop smoking. One, because I started to like it, and two, because of the career path I was about to take going into the military.

The Choir Lesson

I love music and I love to sing. Now, I never said I was great at it, but I love to do it. Music has been a part of my life since I was very young. I remember growing up, The Jackson 5, The Jacksons, and Michael Jackson was pretty much all I used to listen to. I used to sit in front of the stereo system listening to the Michael Jackson Off the Wall album. Quick side note, this album was an extremely well put together album that didn't get the recognition it truly deserved! It did well, but not like it should have. You still hear them play songs from that album to this day. I would be singing along with the album cover open reading the words that were tattooed on the inside of it. I would also have my gray hand-held tape recorder in front of the speaker just so I can have the music on cassette and listen to it later. By this point, I'm sure I have dated myself very well using words like stereo system, album, tape recorder, and cassette. My mom and dad used to see me all the time imitating Michael as I performed around the house. Fast-forward a bunch of years, my mom thought it would be the way to go putting me in the choir at church. Thanks Ma, and I really mean it.

I remember her telling me that I was going to join the choir, and I was telling her how I didn't want to do that. We get to church, she walks me down to the choir room, opens the door and says, "Go ahead." I tell her one last time, "Ma, I don't want to join the choir." "Boy, get in there," she said. I go in the room and she tells the choir director who I was and that I wanted to join the choir. He welcomes me in, I take a seat and we have choir rehearsal. When it was all over, she asks the director how it went and he said, "Yeah, he came right in and started singing and harmonizing–usually when people come in for the first time, I can't get them to sing like that." My mom looks at me and smiles as if to say, "I thought you didn't want to join the choir." All I could do is smile back like, "You got me."

I stayed in the choir for a few years before I joined the US Army, but there was one night that messed me up for a long time. We had just finished a choir rehearsal, and the Spirit of God was in that place big time! I mean the angels came down and the night was anointed! There were people breaking out into praise dance, other people crying, and we were in full worship mode. I absolutely loved it!

When I left rehearsal, I call myself hanging with the older crew of the choir. We went back to one of the guy's apartments. When we walked through the door he goes straight to the TV, turns it on, and low and behold there's porn on the television. My mind was going crazy. I thought to myself, "Didn't we just have a Spirit filled experience in choir rehearsal, and this is what's going on not even an hour after we wrapped up?" But they were letting me hang with them, so I didn't say anything because I wanted to be seen as grown too.

This event actually scarred me, and I never realized to what extent. Seeing what I saw, I began to watch porn and became desensitized to the perversion of it. So yeah, I started to have the 'ask for forgiveness later' mind-set believing that whatever I was doing wasn't that bad. Zero accountability. What in the world was I thinking? Obviously, this is the wrong mind-set to have. Yes, Jesus died and rose to pay the price for our sins so that we may be reconciled back to the Father, but that does not give us a pass to walk in the flesh at will and think we are all good. In fact, this is one of the issues with Christians and why we are sometimes seen in a bad light.

We never know who's watching us when we openly profess Jesus as our Lord and Savior. After doing that, it is important for me to have high accountability because through my actions, I may be leading someone to Jesus every day without knowing. I thank God that he kept me through my stupidity.

I stated earlier that I considered myself to be a good person. I stay out of trouble, do my best to live right, love and honor my marriage and my family, try my best to raise my children correctly, I don't smoke, don't drink, (not that I never have, but I have never habitually drank or smoked), and I do my best to live my life led by the Spirit, but–as I reflect on being a good person, I feel that just being good and doing good works is not enough to get me into the Kingdom of Heaven. I can think I'm good all day, but who does my heart belong to? No man is good, but Jesus and we are made good through Him and Him alone.

CHAPTER 2

Close to the Broken-Hearted

When Bad Things Happen to Good People

Why do bad things happen to "good" people? Why does God allow these things to happen? Why would a loving God allow tragedy to strike where the lives of children are taken? We can go on and on asking these types of questions and the truth is that these types of questions are the ones that keep people from believing in God. Why? Because there is no logical answer that would make us understand why. These are the types of questions that turn our attention away from Him. Not having the answers leaves a bad taste in our mouths about God, relationship with Him, and religion.

The truth of the matter is that God does not cause these things to happen. These bad things that happen to "good" people can be caused, in some cases, by our own decisions, the devil himself, and people with evil in their hearts. You know the ones that believe worshiping Satan is the in thing to do. Those that think being evil is cool. God sees these things that take place, and He cares about the horrible situations that happen. The things that leave you crying your heart out to Him. In the times when you can't feel love for God because you don't understand why he let certain things happen–he still loves you and is so close to you in those moments. God does not cause bad things to happen but if you'll pay close attention to the events that happen after the bad things, you'll see God moving somewhere in the midst. God will take that bad situation and turn it around for good.

What we have to do is be ok with understanding that we're not going to understand everything. How can we fully understand, a Creator who is outside of time and space. The One who spoke all things into existence. Most of us can't really explain the full functions of our iPhone, or how the algorithm code behind social media works. Or try understanding the three-in-one complexity of the Holy Trinity and explaining it for the first time to others so they can understand it. If these things are difficult tasks for us, then how much more difficult is it to understand eternal beings and the works of God. I believe this is why the Bible tells us to "trust" in the Lord with all our hearts, and lean not to our own "understanding." But it guarantees that if we acknowledge God in all things He will make the paths straight.

When bad things do happen, one example of how He turns it for good is that someone's life could be changed to the point where they become one of the great evangelic voices of our time–spreading the gospel of Jesus Christ to many nations. ***Romans 8:28*** says, *"And we know that God causes all things to work together for good to those who love God, to those who are called according to His purpose."* This verse is so important. Notice how it doesn't say "some things," but instead it says, "all things." This, "all things" means just that, ALL THINGS. That means the good, the bad, and the ugly. Things that we don't understand.

Sometimes we can feel the need to have to understand everything that God does and the things that He allows as if they're our plans, or as if we've got the whole world in our hands. When we lose loved ones, we forget that they belong to God in the first place. We take ownership over the people in our lives that are really just borrowed to us. I'm not saying it doesn't hurt–Lord knows that I know that part–I'm just saying that we get mad at God for what we don't understand. Especially when it comes to loved ones, because we're not ready to let go, but God has a perfect purpose and a perfect plan.

My Mother's Smile

My mother and I were very close, and when she got sick it hurt my family very much. We prayed hard, but guess what? God still took her. She belonged to Him. We borrowed her for the time she was on this earth. Did it hurt? Yes. Was I upset? Yes. Was my dad torn to pieces? Of course. It hurt very badly. My mother was a pastor during her short time here on this earth. She loved the Lord dearly and she was very strong in the spirit of God. She was a prophetic woman who loved her family, loved life, and she loved helping people. She could be as goofy as she wanted to be, and that's where I get it from, but then she could be as serious as–I hate to say it–a heart attack, when she needed to be. She loved to laugh and when she did the tip of her nose and her cheeks would get so red. It always makes me smile just thinking about it.

I remember one time while she was battling pancreatic cancer, she was sitting in the car waiting for my dad. I walked up to the door where she was and said, "Mommy, not that I believe anything bad is going to happen to you, but I can't see my life without that beautiful smile." I did my best to have faith that God heard our prayers and that nothing would happen to her. She looked at me with her smiling eyes and said, "You have the same one." As I processed what she said, I later came to the realization that she meant when I needed to see her smile, just look in the mirror, smile, and she will be right there. She died a few months later.

I had to travel all the way from Hawaii to DC to see her. While on the phone with her one time before I was able to get home, I said to her, "Hold on Mommy, I'm coming home." "Ok Baby," she replied in a voice that I barely recognized. After I arrived, she passed five days later while my aunt, (my mom's sister), and I were in the room with her. I watched as she took her last breaths, and in that moment, it seemed as if it were just Mommy and me in that room as I held tightly to her right hand. Memories flooded my brain like a sudden storm that wouldn't cease. As I watched her take her final breath it was, by far, the hardest thing I ever had to do.

The next hardest thing was when I had to go down the hall to get my dad and inform the rest of the family. They were out of the room for a while just to regroup, laugh, and love a little bit. My heart broke as I watched my dad, walk the hallway that seemed like an eternity to get through. His hips developed arthritis; therefore, he was aided by an old black wooden cane— he couldn't walk too fast. This is how he was given the nickname "Turtle." Only I call him that.

As he cried heart-wrenching tears from loosing the one love that had been beside him for thirty-seven years, I silently cried with him. He entered the room, and he walked over to my mom's bed scooping her up into his arms. I think I was still in some kind of shock, but when he slightly lifted her up into his arms, her arms flung back to the sides of her, and I knew for sure that my mom was gone. My Father held my mother with a love grip that was eternal, and sobbed uncontrollably as he gently said, "It's ok Baby, go on and be with the Lord now." When he laid her back on the bed, I looked at her face and noticed that she was slightly smiling. I can only imagine what she saw.

Why did this happen? Did God hear my prayers? Maybe I could have prayed harder. Maybe I should have fasted and prayed even harder. I eventually had to release myself from those thoughts because it wasn't any fault of my own that my mom got sick and died. There was nothing I could've done. It was her time, and God called her home. My mom getting sick wasn't a surprise to God. The Lord knew when and how she would leave this earth when the time came before she was ever born.

We went to my mother's gravesite sometime after she passed, and I kneeled and touched her headstone. As soon as I touched it, I heard my mother's voice very clear saying, "I'm not here. This is just my shell. I will be with you always." I was the only one that went up the five stairs leading to her gravesite but my dad, sister, and I were the ones that went to the cemetery. When I got back in the car, I was a bit reluctant to share what I'd heard, but then I just said, "forget it," and I proceeded to tell them. Their response was that they heard the same exact thing.

Out of us three, I was the one to move on in my mom's footsteps. At least in the same direction. My father and sister's reaction to my mom's passing made them take a step or two away from God for a while. They needed time to process and grieve. Eventually they came back to God–that was just their reaction. The Bible says in Psalm 34:18 that "the Lord is near to the broken hearted and saves those who are crushed in spirit." My dad and sister were truly crushed in spirit at this point because they were there every day with her while I was living in Hawaii. So they were there for her decline and to be honest I don't know how they withstood that. I was there for the last breath, and they tell me they don't know how I withstood that part. I too was crushed in spirit. I just lost my mother–I was very close with my mom. The hardest thing I ever had to do–by far.

Even through our misery, confusion, disbelief, anger, and spiritual blindness, as we push away from God, he draws nearer to us. If you move over two seats, He'll move over toward you one seat. But you say, "Then there's still one seat between us. I thought you said He was close to the broken-hearted?" Yes, He is. That one seat is God giving you a little space to process your feelings and when you're ready he'll move to the next seat closest to you. Aren't you glad that the love of God is way more thoughtful and considerate than we could ever be?

My Uncle's Time

I had an uncle that collapsed and died in his home. While he was in the hospital he couldn't speak or acknowledge our presence. It is to my understanding that he collapsed due to a blood clot. He had been gone for a few minutes before the ambulance came. The paramedics revived him, but maybe a little too late to save him. My uncle was in the hospital for three months before he finally transitioned. He was a great man in my eyes. He and my aunt were married for over 50 years and when asked how their marriage lasted so long, his response was simple. I mean this response was so simple, yet so profound when you think about it. He said, "We just decided a long time ago to agree to disagree." Wow that is deep. If you're married, I invite you to pause right here and take the necessary time you need to think about that. I mean as the saying goes, "there's more than one way to skin a cat." This means there are more than just one way to do things. With that being said, when two people come up with different ways to end up with the same result, it's OK to disagree. No one is wrong you both just think different, as you should, because you are not the same person. You are two different people with two different ways of thinking, so just agree to disagree and keep the train moving.

My aunt is the most beautiful and sweetest soul I know. She's so generous and kindhearted. Together they had two boys that turned into very successful, God-fearing young men. My cousins, whom I have looked up to my whole life, are truly a product of their parents with morals, values, manners, respect, and accountability. While my uncle was in the hospital, countless members of the family, including myself, would go there at different times to visit with him. Hospital visiting hours were 24/7. We would all go up to his room to sit with him, pray for him, sing to him, and to support each other.

One night I was there and had been there for about an hour at this point. I was sitting in a chair while my uncle was asleep. I leaned forward with my elbows resting sharply on my knees and my head resting comfortably in the palms of my hands. The Holy Spirit spoke to me and told me to look at my uncle. Not knowing if he could see me or not, I looked at him and he was looking directly at me. I rose to my feet and walked over to him letting him know that I loved him and that I was there praying for him. I'm sure even though he could not respond he knew how much the family was there showing him love.

Fast forward a month or so, my wife, kids, and I were at Panera Bread eating dinner. I felt something touch my ear. I looked behind me to see if there was anyone there just to find no one standing behind me. In that moment I knew my uncle had passed. By the time we got home, I realized that I had left my phone in the car. I went out to get it and saw that I had missed a few calls. In my mind I was thinking someone was calling to tell me the news and I wasn't wrong. My dad had called me a few times, and my sister called a couple of times. I called my sister back just to hear it from her first because it was my dad's brother that passed and I knew it would be harder to hear it from him.

After I talked to my sister, I called my dad to try and comfort him as best as I could, but what do you really say, right? I had a lot of questions at this point. Why did he still die if everyone was praying so hard? I spent a lot of time in that hospital, and my uncle did not get healed. But I am child of God, right? I was praying so hard, and the Bible says in ***John 14:13-15***, *"Whatever you ask in my name that will I do so that the father may be glorified in the Son. If you ask me anything in my name, I will do it. If you love me, you will keep my commandments."* I love God! Why didn't my prayers work? **Mark 16:17-18** says, *"These signs will accompany those who have believed: in my name they will cast out demons they will speak with new tongues they will pick up serpents and if they drink any deadly poison, it will not hurt them, they will lay hands on the sick and they will recover."*

The Lessons in Loss

I believe in Jesus! I believe that God raised him from the dead! What's going on here? I feel drained in my spirit almost to the level of depression! Am I far from you God? These were the questions that I was wrestling with in my heart at that time. I ended up speaking to my pastor, and he helped me realize that whether God healed my uncle on this side or the other side, he still got his healing. Something else happened too. The other thing that happened was that I had drew very near to God in that time of suffering. In turn God being God, had drawn extremely near to me and my family in our broken heartedness, because He is, in fact, close to the brokenhearted.

CHAPTER 3

Baby Brother

Silver Lining

Baby Boy

Joshua Isaiah Brown. That's the name of my baby brother. He was born on September 25, 1980. This would be the baby of the family and the biggest baby of the siblings weighing in at over 8lbs. I believe I was the runt of the family, but hey, who's keeping track? This guy!

I was seven years old when Joshua was born. A seven-year-old, very active kid, who got into boy things–getting hurt all the time. I was always going to the doctor for something whether it was a cold that usually turned into bronchitis–I got those a lot–or stitches, got those quite often as well. My mom used to make me drag my little sister with me wherever I went. She was two, So, quite naturally she got hurt a lot too. I used to cover up some of it, but some scrapes and bruises I couldn't hide.

I will never forget my first taste of tragedy. It happened on January 15, 1981. It was a Thursday afternoon and there are two things I remember about the school day. First, it was Martin Luther King Jr.'s birthday, and second, I was doing some fingerpainting. My hands were all covered in a forest green colored paint, and I was wearing one of the smocks they gave us so that we wouldn't damage our clothes. As I was smearing the paint over the paper, I hear my name being called to the office for early pick up. I didn't think anything of it, but I was happy to be leaving early. Just when I was walking to the office, I see my dad and my older brother standing in the hallway waiting for me. I noticed my brother was crying. Being the happy kid that I was I smiled and asked what was wrong with him. My dad, standing tall at about 6' 3 ½", slim framed, wearing his army-colored field jacket, looked down at me. That's when I knew something was wrong because his eyes were red and teary. While I'm still smiling, he gives me the news that my baby brother was dead. All I could think about at that point was the night before. I had Joshua on the couch playing with him. I would prop him up in the corner of the couch where the back meets the left arm. I tickled him as he giggled and then slid down to where I had to keep repositioning him. He was a little over three months old.

I remember on the way home I was in the car crying my heart out and looking into the heavens on that rainy day asking God "Why?" We got home, and I went to the sliding door, just off from the kitchen, asking God again, "Why?" I did not understand what was going on. On one hand I wouldn't see my baby brother again in life, and on the other hand my family was wounded deeply, and I couldn't fix it. The frustration over the next few years would really put a dent in the frame of what I found to be my security, my mom and dad. How did this happen you ask? The doctors ruled it Infant Crib Death, but the woman who was babysitting my baby brother was a friend of the family.

The Woman Who Watched Him

There was a woman that my dad knew for a while and we, as a family used to go over to her place. She had two sons and one daughter, and me and my siblings used to play with them whenever we went over to her apartment. They didn't live in the best neighborhood, but I'm not sure if it qualified to be called projects. If it was, I was totally unaware. This woman was the first person to tell me about Adam and Eve, the first humans on earth. I may have been about 5 or six years old when we were spending the night. And while I was lying in bed, she explained that story to me. I remember being so intrigued by the origin story that I believe it is what jump started my love for Jesus.

My mom and dad used to get up early, get us ready for school, and head out to work. While on their way, they would stop off at this lady's apartment and drop Joshua off. On January 15, 1981, she was holding Joshua while feeding him when she noticed that his lips were turning blue. She says that she immediately called 911. I guess by the time they got there he was dead. The problem with this is that she wasn't giving the baby his formula only, but also feeding him grits and eggs, and he just couldn't digest the table food.

My family did forgive the woman, and everyone eventually moved on with their lives, but the scar was extremely thick. I often think of how our relationship would have been. I think it would have been a very close relationship maybe because I've always wanted a baby brother. I know he would have been bigger than me, but I wonder, would he have been a sports guy or a gamer dude. I celebrate his birthday every year silently in my heart. Him and my mom are buried in the same cemetery, so when I go to see my mom, I always go around to the Baby Land section and visit my baby brother.

The Silver Lining

I wonder if the loss of baby brother had anything to do with me having six kids, five of which are boys. I mean, mentally is there a connection? I don't know. I don't see where anything in my mental could produce boys, but it's the number of babies in general that I wonder about. Did the loss of one baby–close to me–result in me producing six of my own? I don't believe I've ever planned to have these many children. I feel like two kids was always my goal. But if for some reason baby brother's death had an everlasting effect on me leading to one girl and five boys than that's just what I call a silver lining. The good things that are produced from the experience of bad things.

I am a firm believer that through everything that happens to us there is something to be learned. What's the take-away? If we don't ask this question, then it could leave us in a state of depression and blame. We could easily blame ourselves, someone else, or even God. Trust me. I know what I am saying is easier said than done, but if we don't understand how to do this then it can leave us stuck. What is there to learn when tragedy strikes? Well, remember we said earlier that "All things work together for good." Believing this is the start of looking for the silver lining.

Often, you'll find that when something bad happens to you somehow the situation always works out. Not by itself–that's God's hand. The situations may not work out right away, and you may have to go through it for a while, but there'll come a time when you see the sunlight again. You will see, if you're looking for it, how everything worked out for the best and maybe even in your favor. Take this very small example. My baby brother's passing and the want for a baby brother has given me two really close friends that are both seven years younger than me. There's the silver lining.

Sometimes it may take years for you to see it, but you must be willing to look for it. Just keep looking. You'll find it. The more willing you are to look, the quicker you'll find it. At the end of the day just know that God has you in the palm of His hand. You just have to trust God. I promise, if you trust Him, it will work out for good. After all, what is the silver lining? It's the sunlight behind the dark cloud. That means behind everything that is dark in your life, God is there ready to push it away and shine His light on you and your situation, so that you can see clearer–so that you can see that He is near to you in your hurt, pain, and lack of understanding.

God is a nurturing, loving, and kind God. He can feel our pain and suffering, but we cannot feel the pain and suffering of Jesus. Even in His horrible death there was a silver lining. One of them was His resurrection, another is the victory that you and I have over sin today because of His death. Every day since the sacrifice of Jesus Christ there have been new people added to the Kingdom of God spreading the Gospel all over the world. That's good news! That's a silver lining!

CHAPTER 4

Recognizing the Blessings

Small Things, Big Blessings

Blessings are all around us and can be found in the simplest things that we take for granted day by day. For instance, have you ever looked at a tube of toothpaste and thought about how blessed you are to be able to have hygiene products in your home? For me that leads to an upward spiral of recognized blessings such as being able to stand in a bathroom, in my house, that has heat and electricity, and then I go to the furnishings in the home. Next, I start thinking about my electronics, like TVs, computers, tablets and phones, my instruments and audio equipment. I'm truly blessed! But the biggest blessing of all would be my wife and my children. I mentioned earlier, "what woman wouldn't want their man to be madly in love with them?"

He Who Finds a Wife

Before I met my wife I was married before. Let's just say that we didn't see eye to eye. That should sum it up in a very small nutshell. Then came Beauty–that's the nickname I gave my wife–staring me right in my face, and she was ready to be loved by me. To say we saw eye to eye would be an understatement. We got a whole vibe going on and she makes me abundantly happy.

We've gone through our ups and downs just like any other couple. We've had our disagreements, we've had our struggles, but all of this we did together because we are in covenant with God. That means something. I am willing to go out on a limb and say that the reason marriages are failing these days is because we are not honoring the covenant between God and our spouse. Everything has to be about us, and what we want, and we forget that marriage is a compromise. I truly believe that if we try to please God in our marriages, they will stand the test of time. I believe we should also check our motives when we decide to marry, because there is a such thing as marrying for the wrong reasons.

The Woman Beside Me

My wife grew up in LA, (Los Angeles, CA), with her mom. She never really knew her father but had seen him a few times in Guatemala. I always felt like this guy was missing out on a beautiful relationship with this beautiful human being. Beauty is so sweet, kind, thoughtful, caring, funny, and slightly stubborn. I truly love everything about her, and I love the way she loves me. This woman has my back for sure! We have gone through some things that made us pray together, laugh together, cry together, and sometimes just sit there and hold each other.

One of my favorite things about Beauty is her love for the Christmas season. She loves to decorate and when I see her in that Christmas spirit it puts me in the same spirit just to know that she is happy. I've always said if I could give her nice vacations, rest and relaxation I would in a heartbeat. There have been times that I have been unemployed, and she has taken the full load on her shoulders. She will always be my little soldier. She is finally retired from the US Army and is now embarking on another career.

Since the first time we started dating she became an instant mom caring for and loving my two children from the previous marriage. There was nothing she wouldn't do for them. When they met, my two oldest kids were at the tender age of four and two at the time. It's been a while. They are both grown now. The biggest blessing in my first marriage was my first two children, Kayla and KJ. The biggest blessing in that divorce is my wife Beauty, and our four children–Jalen, Jonah, Jude, and Jesiah. The one thing I will say about my previous marriage, which is part of my journey, is that whatever valley I went through God was right there with me. Immanuel.

I remember one day when Beauty was sitting in front of the closet putting clothes away, we weren't married at this point, and I asked her, "Do you think you'd make a good wife?" Her response was "I'd make a great wife." She paused for a moment to see if there was anything else following that question, but I just walked away. I was taking time to process what she said. I was ready to lock her down as my woman, but I wanted to be sure, so I waited. The best decision of my life was asking her to marry me. I have so much love, honor, adoration, and respect for this woman. I could go on and on about her, but I think you get my drift.

I guess the message that I really want to drive home here would be recognizing your blessings. There are many things that happen all around us in just a fraction of time, and within these moments there are blessings flowing from person to person. This person's story of blessings may directly affect another's story of blessings. Someone else's blessing could have been related somehow to another's misfortune. Everything is tied together, and one action can start a chain reaction of blessings. In this thought we can unpin the scripture we spoke about earlier, **Romans 8:28**, *"And we know that God causes all things to work* *together for good to those who love God, to those who are called according to His purpose."*

The Chain of Blessings

Let me see if I can illustrate this thought through words and a little bit of imagination. Let's say there is a woman who's feeling a bit insecure lately as she has been listening to her own thoughts that say she's not good enough. She goes to a coffee shop as she does most mornings on her way to work. While in the shop giving her order the man behind the counter gives her a sincerely innocent compliment on the way she looks that day. She smiles and says to the man, "Thank you. You really made my day." She leaves the coffee shop feeling more upbeat and she's got a lot of positive thoughts running through her head now. No doubt, the compliment leads her to be more in a generous mood. For lunch she orders pizza in her office and when the pizza delivery man delivers her order, she tips him a $50.00 bill.

As the pizza delivery man goes on his way, he has another delivery in a poorer neighborhood where he gets robbed by a seventeen-year-old boy. The teenager robs him, but actually, he has no weapon, and the pizza delivery man doesn't get hurt. The teenager flees the scene with the $50.00 bill. The delivery man calls the police, and they catch the teenager. During the arrest, the $50.00 bill falls out of his pocket and on to the ground unnoticed. The police take the young man to the station to in-process him into their system. They asked the young man, "What are you thinking about, being out here trying to rob people?" He replies, "I needed some money to get some milk and bread so my little sister and I could eat while my mom is at work." Fast-forward a few months, the teen only gets a large amount of community service, because he didn't have a weapon, and no one got hurt. While on community service he finds a big brother mentor that leads him to know who Christ is. The result, he gets saved.

Rewinding back to the $50.00 bill, it gets picked up by a homeless man who thanks and praises God for the find. This man has not had a decent meal in five days. With this money that he found he goes and gets that meal, but he also buys food for a homeless friend he made while in his struggle. As for the pizza delivery man, he continued to work that day ending up delivering an order of seven pizzas to a house in a more affluent neighborhood. During this delivery he receives a $100.00 tip, $50.00 more than he lost. He thinks to himself, "God is good."

Remember, all things work together for good to those that love God, and to those that are called according to His purpose. This scenario all started with a compliment. From that compliment, there was a chain reaction of events that ultimately led back to Jesus. The woman was blessed because she wasn't living in an insecure state of mind for that day. The pizza delivery man was blessed because he got a big tip; he may have lost it, but he was protected from harm and then got an even bigger tip. The teenager was blessed, because he thought he was at his last resort. Then God showed him that He cares by pairing him with the big brother mentor who introduced him to Jesus. The $50.00 bill was a blessing because it helped the homeless man and his friend eat well that night. The homeless man was a blessing to his friend by having a compassionate and generous heart to share the blessing he received.

The Blessing in Motion

Recognizing your blessings, even in tough times is vastly important because it allows you to see how God moves in your life even when you think He's far away and not thinking about you. Let me tell you something; God is always thinking about you! God always has you in mind as He is moving throughout this world as the Holy Spirit moved over the surface of the waters in the book of *Genesis 1:2*. You can best believe that God has amazing blessings in store for you, but if you can't even recognize the blessings in the bad times, you will not appreciate them in the good times. You'll begin to think the blessings that occur were done from your own will and not God's will. God is working for good, and when evil acts occur, He's working through them as well. There is always something to be learned through the blessings of God.

CHAPTER 5

I shall Not Want

Psalm 23

Psalms 23:1-3 says, *"The Lord is my Shepherd, I shall not want. He makes me lie down in green pastures; He leads me beside quiet waters. He restores my soul; He guides me in the paths of righteousness for His name's sake."*

My two favorite Christian groups at that time, came together on a collaboration album called Old Church Basement. You probably heard of Elevation Worship and Maverick City Music. Well on this album there's a song called Shall Not Want featuring Chandler Moore, written by him, Chris Brown, Naomi Raine, and Pastor Steven Furtick. The lyrics start off like this, "Will You be my light when I cannot see, and when I can't take another step, Lord, would You carry me? And When I've lost my fight will You be my strength? Will You set me a table in the presence of my enemies? I shall not want..." This song resonates with me, and I'll share with you why.

The Struggle

I mentioned earlier that there were times when I didn't have a job and my wife took on the load herself. She did it without complaint too. Just another reason why I love her so much. Well, things were really hard as I was trying to find my way outside of military life. Oh, I guess this is a good time to mention that I was nine years active-duty Army and thirteen years Air Force Reserve. While in the Army I had a steady check coming in, but when I got out, I had to make the money come in steadily which was a rollercoaster of a journey. Every time we had to PCS, (which stands for Permanent Change of Station), I had to find another job. In 2010 we moved from Arizona to Maryland.

As I was looking for a job I first worked with my friend, (more like a brother), in his business of janitorial services. He had this business for quite some time, and it was going great for him and his family. I worked for him part-time for a couple of months making $600.00 a month. One night I had finished cleaning one of the churches out in Virginia. When I got back to Maryland I had to make a stop at a CVS Pharmacy. Getting ready to get out of the car, I stopped and just sat there for a minute. It was after two o'clock in the morning–I was dog tired. I started to think about my life and wondered why it was so hard for me to find a decent job with the background that I had. I was traveling about an hour and a half in the middle of the night to clean a church receiving $600.00 a month for pay, and I really depended on that money. I was grateful for the help–I just knew I could do better.

At that moment I began to pray and cry uncontrollably. I was asking God what was wrong with me and where did I fail. It didn't help that I was missing my mother too. The person that I felt could make all of this make sense to me, but God heard my cry.

The Provision

Not long after that I got hired for two jobs on the same day. The gym on the military installation and Guitar Center. It was a sweet gig because neither of the jobs paid a lot, but here's where it was so convenient. The gym paid about $9.50 per hour and the hours were 4:45am to 1:45pm. After I got off the gym job I could go home, take a nap, and then go work the Guitar Center job that paid $7.50 plus commission where I'd work from 5 pm to 9:30 pm. That had me at $17.00 an hour. It was a sweet set up for me that I was so thankful to God for. Then it happened. Something had to mess everything up. The manager at the gym and I had an agreement for me to work early mornings. He then changed his mind, because he was getting ready to fire someone on the afternoon to evening shift and wanted to put me in their place. Prior to this happening I had two people that kind of belittled me for working at the gym. That didn't feel good at all. One guy looked down on me for passing out towels, and the other actually said the words "What a waste." They didn't know my story or who I was, or where I came from. The first one just straight up belittled me and the other one was believing that I could be doing more–he was absolutely correct!

Back to the gym manager–he tells me that he needs me in the evenings. I told him that I had another job in the evenings and then he gave me an ultimatum. He says, "You need to figure it out. Either you're going to work at the gym or Guitar Center." I was thinking about it hard and even though the gym paid more I took the job that paid less. I chose Guitar center over the gym. I went to school for Audio Engineering, so it only made sense for me to work at Guitar Center in the Pro Audio section. When I told the gym manager my answer, he was hot! I had to go in the next morning with my letter of resignation and when I went to shake his hand and thank him for the opportunity, this guy couldn't even shake my hand. I stood there and, in my mind, I said, "WOW!" Side note: Never make business personal because just when you think it's the other party burning the bridge, it could actually be you burning that bridge.

So, there I was–working solely at Guitar Center for $7.50 per hour plus commission. It would be here that God would show his favor over my life. It seemed like everything I made at that music store went right back to them. I was buying something every night when I got off. Beauty gave me a room in the house, and I was slowly but surely building a music studio there. One of the managers liked me, and the assistant manager–maybe not so much. I kind of got that vibe from him like even he didn't know why he didn't like me. Sometimes when God's favor is upon you, others will look at you trying to figure out how you're winning when you should be at the bottom getting walked over. HALLELUJAH!!! Take a moment because that's somebodies praise break right there!

The policy was that you had to be there for at least six months before you could make purchases over $299.00. I walked in one day trying to buy this piece of equipment that was $699.00, and it just so happened that the manager that liked me was not there but on a business trip. At this point, I was unaware of the policy. The assistant manager that I thought didn't like me was at the register and he's the one that let me know about the policy. He told me that unless I could get the top manager to say it was ok then I couldn't buy this piece of equipment. He also reminded me that the top manager was out of town. I told him, "Ok, give me a second." I called the top manager on my cell phone and gave the other manager the phone. During their conversation I saw the assistant manager's face change from confident in his answer to why does this new guy have so many privileges? God's favor, that's why! The top manager told him to go ahead and let me purchase the equipment. I never had another issue buying anything out of there again.

Dan the Man

God's still moving. Someone walked in the store one day and I sold him a set of speakers. His name was Jacob. He was wearing a shirt that was advertising a small contracting company. I asked him about it and if they were hiring. He said yes, so, I gave him my information, and I got hired for a different job working in a warehouse from 7:30am to 3:30pm making $17.00 and hour. This job was really flexible and almost eerily safe. Some guy called me for an interview. He wanted to meet me at a McDonald's on the corner in Arnold, MD. I met with him and the whole interview we talked about a common interest–music. Both guys would become very close friends of mine because we were all tied up into music.

The one who would interview me, his name was Dan and he would be my manager. Dan was a down-to-earth type of person with strong morals and values and loved his parents and family. He was an older guy than I was at the time. He would always talk about sports and music because he grew up playing baseball and the trumpet in school. He would always have his feet up on the desk while he was on the computer at work. He said it relieved some pain that was in his lower back. We became very close. I met his family and cared about them as if they were my very own. I worked there for three years with three more people, one being Dan's sister Dale, Carlos and Jerry. We all worked very well together and got things done. Maybe a little too well because there was an awful amount of downtime. That's when Jerry and I would go jump in the van and hit the 7-11 or the Wawa. I think that's what had me stagnant for so long. When I say that, I mean I felt safe even though I wasn't making that much money. But yes, it was more than I was making at Guitar Center.

One morning we came into work and Dan was late. When he finally came in, he was distressed and very sharp and to the point. This wasn't his normal character, so I thought we were in trouble when he said he had to talk to us. When he finally spoke, we found out that his youngest son had some type of cancer. I believe he was only thirteen. I had compassion on Dan as did Carlos, a very wise and spiritual man with a very different past. I hugged Dan and then he let the tears that he'd been holding onto, in an effort to be strong for his family, flow. I prayed for him and wondered what was God up to at this point? Deep down I knew that Dan's son would be just fine though. He informed us that there would be a lot of days that he would be late or that he would leave early, or maybe not show up at all, due to appointments with his son. We had his back and we–Carlos, Jerry, Dale and me–kept the ship rolling. After a while of being out of school and losing his hair, Dan's son recovered fully with a better head of hair, a desire for school, and a social life. You can't ask for much better than that.

The "But God" Moments

My job consisted of me driving this big box truck to make deliveries to the other side of the bridge at the Naval Academy in Annapolis, MD. After taking the truck in for repairs we waited a while to get it back. When I went to pick the truck up, I noticed immediately that something was wrong with the steering. The steering column felt loose and rubbery as making my way back to the jobsite. I told the proper people about the issue, but it seemed like nothing was done to resolve it. About a year and a half later I'm getting ready to take the truck to Ft. Meade, MD on a clear and sunny day to do a turn-in of old equipment. As I started to drive the Holy Spirit spoke to me telling me to take the back roads instead of the highway. Being obedient, I took the back roads and reached my destination.

After the mission was complete, I took about an hour for lunch and then it was time to get back on the road. I figured, ok since I took the back roads to get here, I'm going to take the back roads to get back to Annapolis. I left the military installation and about four minutes into my drive I hit a slight bump, and I heard something snap or pop. I continued driving. As the road is starting to bend to the left, I slightly turn the wheel following the direction the road was setting and got no response from the vehicle. The road is bending more and I'm turning the wheel more—still no response. Then I grabbed the wheel and spun it all the way to the left and there was absolutely no response from the truck. I literally watched the steering wheel spin as if I was a contestant on "The Price is Right," and then the Holy Spirit snapped me out of my state of shock and told me to brake. The truck stops. I put the emergency brake on and got myself safely to the side of the road where I dropped to my knees in broad daylight, threw my hands in the air and began to cry and thank God for sparing my life. If I had gotten on the highway, the route I usually take for this trip, I would have been doing sixty to seventy mph and could have killed myself or someone else with this uncontrolled box truck. My kids were in school that day, and my wife was in Texas on a business trip. This could have gone another way, but God... Have you ever had a "but God" moment in your life? Oh, I've had quite a few of those moments in my life.

My time was getting short working for this contract company. After this incident I believe they could tell how upset I was at their lack of action toward the repair of this truck. They ended up asking me if I'd like to move to a different job within the same company. I agreed. There was a $2.00 increase, but I wouldn't really see it due to the commute and the parking situation. I went anyway, and it wasn't that bad only, I was trying to get a permanent government job and got passed over for it. Then I saw that there was a contract job opening on the military installation where my wife worked, and it just so happened to be in the same unit where she worked as well. I applied for that job with no mention of her name. I got the job. During the phone call I said, "I was at least looking for $50,000.00 a year." and they said, "OK we're going to go ahead and give you $60,000.00," because that is what I put on my application.

So now I'm stoked! Super excited that the Lord has blessed me this way. After about six months the contract is changing over, and some other company wins the bid. Everyone on the contract is worrying because they may or may not have a job with this new company. Me, I wasn't worried a bit. I had a deep peace about it. The new company takes over and they're calling people to see if they would stay with their new pay. They get on the phone with me, and they announce my position, and they said, "This job pays $85,000.00 a year, will you take it." "$85,000.00?" I asked.

His response, "Yes."

"Mmmmm, I guess I'll take it."

"Ok, Good. Well, this was a quick negotiation," with a slight chuckle from the negotiator.

The only thing I could do at that point was praise God, because he had taken me from working part time making $600.00 a month to the gym job and Guitar Center, to just Guitar Center where I was able to sell speakers to Jacob, landing a job with Dan for $17.00 per hour, to working with my wife making $88,400.00 a year by the time the job ended. Normally I wouldn't put all these numbers out there like that, but it is necessary to show how God works. Keep in mind I was being faithful in tithes and offering and working in the church as the Audio/Visual team lead.

The Shepherd's Hand

All of this was to illustrate how God already knew my needs. He used me to grow relationships so strong with the people I was working with, and to be some comfort to them in a time of need. I never needed anything I didn't already have or have access to. Each time I needed a job He had one lined up for me because He was working behind the scenes. I shall not want. When I needed breaks, He gave them to me before I even knew I needed them. He makes me lie down in green pastures; He leads me beside quiet waters. He is my Shepherd, and I shall not want.

CHAPTER 6

Trusting God

Proverbs 3

Who do you put your trust in? Is it people? Is your trust deposited into another human being? Do you trust in money or material possessions? The Bible speaks on who your trust should be in as well. ***Proverbs 3:5-6*** says, *"trust in the LORD with all your heart and do not lean on your own understanding. In all your ways acknowledge Him, and He will make your paths straight."* I know it's hard not to lean on your own understanding, and for most people, it's hard trying to put your trust in someone you can't see. God knows this as well, and therefore, Jesus said in ***John 20:29***, *"...Blessed are those who have not seen and yet have believed."*

When Trust Hurts

We would love for everything to go our way, just the way we planned things, ourselves, without inviting Jesus into our plans. But that's not always the case, is it? My wife and I planned to have a baby a few years back. She did get pregnant, and we were expecting. We were pretty excited as we anticipated the arrival of the new baby. We went to the first appointment, and they gave us a sonogram picture of our little bundle of joy on the way. We had some close friends of ours–a married couple–that were about to have their first baby in the same time frame as us. They had told us that they were expecting, and we were super excited for them. Then we told them that we were too. Everyone was just so happy and cheerful. About eight weeks into it my wife started bleeding a bit. She finally got an appointment to see the doctor just to learn that the child was not alive. I was at work that day while she was at her appointment.

She called me when it was over, and I eagerly asked her how it went. That's when she started crying and told me that the doctors said, "the baby stopped at about eight weeks." I couldn't even focus on work anymore. I had to leave abruptly, and when I got home, I was just crying and telling God how much I trust Him. "I trust you Lord, I trust you," is what I kept saying over and over again. What was God up to in this moment that I had no control over? All I could do was trust God and look and listen for silver lining lessons. What I walked away with was that He was in control and His timing is perfect. We had two more babies after that stressful situation.

How was I able to trust God that way when it seemed that my life was turned upside down momentarily? I was able to trust Him that way by letting go of what I wanted, knowing that what God wants for us was better than we could ever imagine. He's so kind to us. Maybe in His timing it wasn't right for us, and we just couldn't see it. He knew our desire to have a child and said, "Soon, but not yet." We must trust that the Lord's promises are yes and amen.

Faith in the Fire

My wife's has freckles on her face and body. More on her body than face. She had one come in on the right side of her face, just below her eye and beside her nose. We joked about it all the time calling it her beauty mark. One day the mole started to swell up like a bump under her skin. Later, on another day, as she was washing her face it began to bleed. She scheduled a doctor's appointment and when she was seen, she was hit with some disturbing news about the beauty mark. She was diagnosed with having a skin cancer called Basal Cell Carcinoma or BCC. When she got home and told me the news, we both cried and once again I held her and told God, "I trust you."

We prayed about it and found a peace that calmed our spirits. We found out that it was treatable, but they had to cut a piece of skin from my wife's face. The scar healed nicely, and now we know that we must keep an eye out for her freckles and moles to make sure that they aren't the cancerous cells. The one thing that keeps us so full of faith and trust in the Lord is knowing that the stories we read about in the Bible are not just any old stories, but they are stories of the way God moves, and knowing that God is the same yesterday, today, and forever more gives us the security to trust Him. Like the song says, "If He did it before He can do it again!"

The Trust Blueprint

There are many stories in the Bible that demonstrate trust in God. We can look at Abraham and the way He trusted God with the life of His son Isaac–the promised son. There's Daniel in the lion's den or Joseph's imprisonment. One story that I love is about Shadrach, Meshach, and Abednego. No matter how much their lives were threatened by the king of Babylon, (Nebuchadnezzar), who besieged Jerusalem, they would not fall down and worship the golden image. Nebuchadnezzar had all three of them thrown in a fiery furnace. They trusted that God would save them from the furnace, but they believed that even if God didn't deliver them, He was still always able to do that and so much more.

After they were thrown into the furnace the king looked inside. Nebuchadnezzar saw four images instead of three and he said that the fourth looked like a son of the gods. How great was their trust and faith to say that even if God doesn't deliver us, we know that He is able?

How is it that we can put our trust a chair that we've never sat on, but we can't put our trust in our Maker? How is it that we can trust food that someone else cooked, people we don't even know, but we can't trust the Creator of the Heavens and the Earth? Why is it that we can trust other drivers on the highway driving inches away from us, but we can't trust the God who woke us up this morning? We trust Facebook and Instagram more than we trust God. You don't believe me? I'll prove it. Many people go straight to their phones as soon as they wake up in the morning or go to bed at night. We do this before we ever acknowledge God's presence in our lives. Our phones have become our god, because we always have it in our hands, it speaks to us through all the different apps that are just begging to be tagged.

Have you ever picked up your phone to do something and then got sidetracked by all the apps that are on that phone? I mean you totally forget what you were going to do on the phone but there's an old trusty app that you like that just distracted the mess out of you. We have our whole lives in our phones, and we trust them to keep our information and secrets safe. One thing you can trust with those phones though is that it will surely die on you. Let it not be close to a charger and the battery life will fail you. But what I've found is that God will never fail you and He can never die. You should always trust that.

We must be more aware of our Father's presence in our lives. He is Holy, and we are not. He is sovereign and we are not. Why do we take his presence for granted? We do know that if God told us not to wake up in the morning that we wouldn't, right? A lot of us use our alarms on our phones to wake us up in the morning. Sometimes we can mis-set the alarm and not wake up at the desired time, but God can make you sleep and not wake up again, ever! God deserves your trust because He loves and cares, truly, about us. He is concerned with what concerns you. He is the friend that sticks closer than a brother. When you hurt, God wants to make you feel better, but He also uses your hurt to teach your heart how to trust and love. You can trust God because He has your soul in mind. He loves you so much that He sent Jesus to take your place before death so that you can be with Him in Heaven and have relationship with Him. God is so good; He deserves our trust.

A Good Father

There are going to be times that we just don't understand who, what, when, where, why, and definitely not how, but if we trust in God and His plan, and in His timing, He will surely take care of us and all of our needs because He is a good Father. Just as a parent must watch over their children, God watches over us even more so. Sometimes that means that things are not going to go the way we want or think they should go, but you can best believe they will turn out a whole lot better than we could've imagined by God's grace. If we trust in the Lord with all our heart, and do not lean on our own understanding, and in all our ways acknowledge Him, He will make our paths straight. All you have to do is trust Him as much as you trust that chef in the back of the restaurant, cooking your food, or even the waiter who brings it out to you.

Immanuel in the Valley

CHAPTER 7

2020 – Matters of the Heart

The Kobe Effect

It was December of 2019. Everyone heard of COVID 19 but had no idea that it would be the pandemic that it became. Some take the liberty in blaming the president at the time for downplaying the situation. On that note, my opinions will remain my own, because this book is not about anything political. A little heads up would've been cool though, I'm just saying. However, this year actually started horribly in the first month of the year.

We had just gotten to Belgium after being stationed in Maryland for a little over eight years. I remember lying in the hotel bed with my wife and my baby boy Jude when my older son Jalen comes in the room and says, "Did you hear about Kobe Bryant?" I said, "What about him?" Then my son replies, "He was killed in a helicopter crash." "No he wasn't! Where is your source coming from?" I replied. I was thinking that it was some kind of joke, but then He said that his source was from my oldest son KJ. At that point I knew it was true. We all love basketball, and Kobe, so I knew he would have heard the real news still being in the States and all.

I immediately turned on the news channels, but it took a while for the news to start filtering in. My heart was heavy with the weight of this news. As the story started to unfold and I found out that his baby girl was on the helicopter too I was done. I started thinking about his wife Vanessa and the baby girls, and how Vanessa had to be devastated. I was extremely heavy with grief and pain, not to mention I had just found out days before about the death of a church member named Leo. He had mentioned to me that he felt as though he was not good enough and that he didn't matter. He was an older gentleman that I cared for deeply. I prayed for Vanessa and the seven other families whose loved ones perished in that helicopter crash that day. Then, here comes March.

During this month everything starts getting locked down and curfews are set in place. In Belgium, the government was not letting anyone in or out of the country. They had curfews in place and police on the streets to enforce them. The streets were eerily empty, and every where we went during the day people's face was covered up. I could only think to myself, "What in the heck is going on across the world?" When I looked at the news to check in on the USA everyone's face was covered up, but then

I started to notice the push back of the people from wearing the mask, but people were dying left and right. Frontline workers were getting burnt out, hospitals were running out of space all across the world, there weren't enough face masks for the demand. We were most definitely in the middle of a global pandemic. Where a lot of people got to experience working from home, I was one that still had to go into work, and I thank God that I didn't catch the Corona virus. I was still doing my best to stay safe though. 2020 was so bad that it seemed as though everyone was just trying to make it out of that year without dying.

The Warning Shot

October 25, 2020, I woke up early that morning, got dressed and went into the garage where we built our little home gym because the public gym was closed. I got a good workout in and then gathered the family in to watch a sermon on TV. It was Pastor Steven Furtick from Elevation Church. When the sermon was over, and Pastor Steven was giving his call to Jesus, I felt an immense pain in my chest. I walked to my bedroom, and I fell to my knees and threw my arms over the bed. This pain lasted for about twenty-five to thirty minutes. My wife came in the room, and I told her what happened and then I cried and said, "I don't want to die," as I hugged her tightly. I didn't go to the hospital because the pain had gone away. I thought to myself, "I am not touching those energy drinks anymore." So, I was self-monitoring after that.

The Widow Maker

November 28, 2020, it was late in the afternoon, and my wife and I were in the garage digging for the stored Christmas boxes. The pain that I had felt a month earlier came back and this time it did not go away. My wife said, "Go sit down for a minute." I sat down and the pain was only getting stronger. I told her, "Hey we have to go to the hospital." She stops what she's doing, but I'm kind of rushing her because it felt like she was moving too slow. I believe I was just getting anxious though. While I was in the car trying to keep myself together, I had pain that moved to my jaw. Beauty kept trying to keep me calm and I thank God it was working.

The hospitals were getting overcrowded with COVID cases. I went inside and tried to explain, over the language barrier, what was happening to me. They stuck the swab in my nose, and I guess they were waiting for the results, but I began to get more anxious. I got off the bed and went into the hallway sweating profusely, at this time, and asked if someone would please help me and give me some kind of medicine for the pain.

They came back in the room, took some blood, and then gave me medicine through a tube and said they had to wait three hours for the results of the blood work. Three hours went by, and I went out in the hallway again trying to find someone that would tell me something. As I stepped in the doorway the doctor was walking pass the door, I stopped him to ask him what was going on, then he came into my room and asked me how I felt, I told him, "My chest hurts really bad." He responded with, "Your heart has suffered…" In so many words I had a heart attack which technically was my second one. They got me ready and rushed me over to another hospital where I would get a stint placed in my artery and spend five days in the hospital. Later I would find out that the artery that was blocked is known as the ***"Widow Maker,"*** or the left anterior descending artery, (LAD). ***Steven Brown***, *(May 2020), stated in a WebMD article, "Heart attacks can be deadly, and the widow maker is one of the deadliest kinds. It can happen suddenly when a key artery that moves blood to the heart gets almost or completely blocked. Without emergency treatment, you may not survive. Despite its name, the widow maker strikes women, too."*

The Knockout

December 16, 2020, I had just woken up that morning from sleeping on the couch, because I couldn't lay in the bed just yet. I was afraid to sleep, so I would stay up all hours of the night. Well, this particular morning, I got up and walked over to the dinning room table. I was getting ready to take my meds, which by the way, I had never taken any medication prior to the heart attack, when I felt an impact on my head. I had passed out and hit my head on the floor. My head was cut in the back. The impact was that strong.

I rolled over and tried to call my wife because my phone was on the floor charging. She answered but we got disconnected. I looked around and my vision wasn't clear. While I'm crawling to the kitchen to call my wife again from the house phone, it rings. I remember I touched the phone to answer it, but then I passed out again only to wake up to my mother-in-law shaking my arm and calling my name trying to wake me up. As I was coming to, I felt her wiping sweat from my head. After that whole episode, I was pretty hungry. I looked in the cabinet to prepare a bowl of cereal and eat while I watched TV. The name of the cereal was Life. I can't make this stuff up. That's that breakfast you eat when you're trying to live apparently. Just kidding—it was all we had at the time.

I had absolutely no clue as to what had happened to me. I told my wife I was ok, but she insisted that I go to the ER again. I got admitted again and this time I would spend fourteen days in the hospital as I waited for my procedure of getting an ICD (Implantable Cardioverter-Defibrillator) inserted in my chest.

Positive Vibes Only

While I waited, I was in a room by myself, but we had to get permission for my wife to be able to see me as I was admitted over the Christmas season. Because of COVID, hospital visitation was not recommended, but there were case-by-case exceptions. I thank God my wife was able to see me during the change in the hospital policies, even if for a little while. She would come and bring me certain things that I wanted like my computer, interface, headphones, and microphone. You know the typical things people need while they're in the hospital. Seriously though, I took the time that I was in there to write and somewhat produce a song for Beauty. The song wasn't good at all, but I don't think that was the important thing. This was one way to take my mind off what was going on for real. When my wife would come to see me, the nurses told her she had ten minutes, but since I was the only one in the room she would stay as long as she wanted to, and they wouldn't say anything to her. It felt good just to sit and talk to the other half of me. To be able to hold her, smell her, touch her, and laugh with her gave me a sense of home and comfort that I really needed in that moment.

I remember she came up to the hospital on Christmas day with an ugly Christmas sweater, some Christmas cards from the boys, and gifts for me. I felt the love from my wife, but I also felt her pain because I knew that she would keep it together for me while she was with me, then let it all out on her way home from the hospital. Whenever I knew she was coming I made sure that I was up and walking around so she wouldn't see me in the bed. I needed to be up and walking around too, because I didn't want to be confined to the bed and the vitals machine.

Beauty's presence gave me an energized motivation and enthusiasm. Sometimes just being around someone you love can make a real difference in your healing process. I feel for those who had loved ones in the hospital dealing with COVID by themselves, because I really believe that in some cases, people may have healed faster or may have lived if they had the extra motivation of family with them. I don't know for sure–it's just a theory. As much as I would love for that to be true trying to contain that virus was no easy feat.

I was unexpectedly positive about my situation up to this point. I knew that God had me and that it was no surprise to Him that I was going through this ordeal. I was believing that my suffering was for a reason, and that God would bring me through it and one day I would see what that reason was. I still believe that to this day. I surrounded myself with positive music and if I spoke to anyone on the phone, I needed them to have positive vibes only. "No negativity," was my motto. During this time negative vibes were not going to do anything for me in my healing process, and the truth is that they don't help a situation anyway. You cannot grow, (growing being the positive), if you're constantly surrounding yourself with negative minded people. The way I saw my situation was that I was still alive, and if Jesus wanted to take me from this earth He would have.

Too Close for Comfort

Christmas came and went, and I was still there in the hospital. Prior to being moved to the room to myself, I was in the room next door. I was in there alone at first, then I had a roommate that came in. This guy was coughing and just being obnoxiously loud on the phone while talking to his family and friends. To say I was annoyed would be an understatement. The next day I see this guy getting dressed and leaving my room. I thought to myself, "He must be good to go." Come to find out, this guy had the Rona! I was extremely upset, because they put him in the room with me without knowing his status first of all, but then they got him out of the room way before ever notifying me of what was taking place. It took a while for them to move me to another room so that they could disinfect the former room.

This would be the first of two times the nursing staff put me in the same room with a COVID positive person. The lack of communication being in the Belgian hospital was very discouraging. But God kept me even through that scare. Three days after Christmas I received my procedure where the ICD was placed in my chest. The operation was a success, and I went home approximately two days later.

Imperfect Timing

It was late. Everyone was sleeping already and I was the last one to go to bed. I took a shower and got myself ready to hit the sack. I finally fell asleep and suddenly I was awakened to a very rapid heartbeat. I wasn't doing anything but sleeping, so I got up and checked my heart rate with a device that my sister had bought me. I put the device on my finger, and my heart rate read one hundred twenty-two bpm. This scared me because not only was my heart beating way too fast, but I was feeling palpitations as well. Beauty was sleep, so I had to wake her up to take me to the hospital. I know I should have called 911, but for some reason I felt better alerting my wife first. We joke about that all the time.

(Side note). On one occasion we joked about it because I had gone to the gym, and she knew where I was. After the gym I went to Walmart, but when I got there, I thought to myself, "I'm only going in for a few minutes, so I'm going to leave my phone in the car." Beauty called me two times while I was in the store then she called her mom to see if I was at the house. By the time I got back to the car my phone was ringing and it was Beauty again. She was worried about me because my last location that she knew of was the gym. I told her that she knew if something would have happened, I would have called her before 911. We both laughed and agreed that I should be calling 911 in the event of something really happening. One thing I didn't mention earlier is that while we were dealing with my heart issues, Beauty was pregnant with our last baby. You can imagine the stress on her.

After I woke her up, she got dressed and took me to the hospital ER. Once we arrived, there was no one manning the front desk. Finally, I found someone. I did my best to let them know what was going on with me, because they didn't have an English-speaking person there that night. They put me in the hospital bed and hooked me up to the vitals machine. My wife walks right in from the reception area because no one was there manning the reception desk. With me included, there may have been three people in the ER that night. The other two people were the nurses and then also my wife, of course. At this point something is going very wrong with me. I felt hot, I was losing my sight as if I'd somehow entered a tunnel of sorts. I was losing consciousness and was trying to communicate that to the nurse. I looked at the vitals machine and found my heart rate. It went from one hundred twenty-two to one hundred twelve. The nurse is not understanding me as I kept saying, "I'm getting light-headed." I looked at my wife and told her that I loved her, because I felt as though I was slipping away. Inside my body I could feel that I was on the verge of losing my bowels.

Now my heart rate is dropping rapidly. The nurse is looking at the machine not really responding yet, but then the machine numbers dropped from one hundred twelve to six. Not one hundred six, but six. The machine started beeping erratically and the nurses started to react! They frantically tilted my bed head down so the blood could rush to my head, I'm guessing so I wouldn't lose consciousness. When all of that was over, there I stayed for the rest of the night in that position–head downward. In the morning, they transported me back to the hospital that I had been to twice before. The diagnosis was some sort of arrythmia and I needed a cardiac ablation. The cardiologist would make an appointment for March 16, 2021, which didn't seem to far away at all until the next arrythmia episode.

March 4, 2021, around 1:30am, I had just got in bed after taking a shower again. As I tried to go to sleep, I was interrupted by a different arrythmia and palpitation. I lay on my side with my ear folded in so I could hear my heartbeat and what I heard, I couldn't believe. I woke Beauty up again and had her put her ear to my chest to see what she heard. She said, "You definitely need to go to the hospital." My heart was beating, but it didn't have a rhythm to it at all. It was a very sporadic heartbeat. We get up, get dressed, and headed out the door.

During this time the streets are empty because there was another curfew put in place due to COVID still. We get to the hospital, and my heart didn't do anything weird while they were checking me and pulling up a printout of my heart activity. The nurse came back to me and said, "Everything is fine." Then my heart started doing a number again. I said, "It's happening again right now." She looked at the machine I was hooked up to and turned it away from me so only she could see it. I understood why. If I saw the machine tracking my heartbeat looking anything like I was feeling I probably would've freaked out.

She took another printout as it was happening and consulted with the doctors. In the morning my cardiologist came into my room and talked with me. He explained what was happening and reminded me that I had an appointment for a cardiac ablation on March 16th. I looked at the doctor square in his eyes and said, "The 16th huh?" The way I said it was almost as if to say, "I don't think I'm going to make it until then." He knew what that look meant and told me that he would do his best to try and get the appointment moved up to the 8th which was the very next Monday. They gave me a medicine they didn't want to leave me on because it was more so for elderly people to regulate their heartbeat. There I sat in the hospital over the weekend waiting for Monday.

Day of the Procedure

March 8, 2021, early in the morning they get me ready to go to the surgery room. I have prayed up to this point that God will bring me on the other side of this procedure. When it was all over, I realized how much trust I put in the doctors when I would get certain procedures done not even taking into consideration the number of things that can go wrong during the operation. But I will not live in fear, I will trust in the Lord my God.

I'm lying in the bed waiting to be taking to the back for my operation, and I keep hearing them say my last name and COVID. Quite naturally, I'm wondering what's going on and is someone going to come and tell me something. They finally roll me to the back. They transfer me to my operating table and began to put wires on me and suddenly, they stopped. What is going on? Why did they just stop? All the nurses, doctors, and anyone else helping, walked away from me and they all went into another room and had a conversation about me having COVID. They finally came back to the operating table and continued to hook me up to the necessary machines. "Is everything OK?" I asked. They told me everything was fine, and they continued step by step with the procedure.

They started to administer the anesthesia, but I didn't fall asleep as quick as I thought, maybe I was fighting it a little bit. Hours go by, but obviously I can't feel the amount of time I'm being operated on. Then finally, they wake me up and start asking me how I feel. For some reason my sinuses seemed to be draining like crazy, so I let them know. They put me in the recovery room, and another doctor came by and asked me how I felt. I again explained, "My sinuses are draining heavily, but other than that I'm ok." Then the doctor tells me that during the procedure I had to be shocked a few times and on one of those shock treatments my body reacted some kind of way. My face hit the lamp above me breaking my nose. This explains what I thought were my sinuses draining. I was swallowing blood from the nose break.

An ENT doctor came to visit me next, and she repaired my nose while I was still in the recovery area, which was an open bay separating patients by partitions. I was kind of in disbelief and couldn't wait to speak to my wife. She couldn't wait to speak to me either. By the time I got out of surgery it was close to 3:00pm. My wife had been calling the hospital trying to get a status update on me but felt like she was getting the run-around. I finally get to my room about 4:15 – 4:30pm. I called Beauty at work, and she just starts going in telling me how worried she was about me and how she called the hospital, and they would tell her bits and pieces of my status and whereabouts. I let her talk because it was really good to just hear her voice at this point.

When she finished, I just mumbled the words, "They broke my nose," and she got extremely quiet. At this point she wanted to FaceTime, so we did. She saw me and with no exaggeration I looked like death. My nose was bandaged up, and I still had dried up blood on my face running from my nose through my beard. My lips were super thin. She took a picture of the FaceTime call, and I literally look like I had died and came back. They didn't say it like that but that's what it looked like.

Suddenly, she started to show frustration in the hospital for the way the whole thing went down. She sounded really concerned and angry for not telling her upfront what happened. Truth of the matter is, I should have been out of that procedure way earlier. It started at 8:30 in the morning. They said they would be done around 12:00 or 1:00 pm. My wife didn't get to speak to me until around 4:30 pm. In her anger and frustration, I could tell she was trying to keep calm for the baby too. Beauty has always had this quiet strength about her.

After a while we got off the phone and I had the chance to reflect on what had just taken place. I lie back in the bed with just one light on over my head. I grabbed my phone and played the song Isaiah's Song by Maverick City. It's at this moment I realized that the Lord had saved me and brought me through this horrible situation. Even the nose break was necessary in my opinion, because it gave me something else to focus on other than what was going on in my chest. I had to concentrate on breathing and trying to eat and swallow rather than wondering how my heart was holding up.

San Antonio Bound

Beauty was fed up with the way things were done in Belgium concerning my situation, and there was also the language barrier, so she put in for a compassionate reassignment, which sent us to San Antonio, Texas. We had always kept Texas in mind as one of the places we would settle down because it was eighteen to twenty hours each way to both of our hometowns–Los Angeles and Washington, D.C. When it came down to it, she put three different places on her list of where she wanted to go–San Antonio being the first, then Maryland, and finally Georgia. The branch managers said no to all those locations and gave her the options of Washington state, North Carolina, and Ft. Hood

Texas. After we talked it over, she chose North Carolina. We got ourselves set on North Carolina becoming home when all of a sudden, the branch management team calls her back and said they had an opening in San Antonio, Texas at Ft. Sam Houston. They asked her if she still wanted it and she said yes, and so here we are.

I started getting acquainted with the necessary doctors, but the day I went to see my cardiologist, all the computers were down, so we didn't get to go into depth about my health. I got two or three more appointments scheduled with the cardiologist, but they all got cancelled. It was beginning to become a frustrating situation all over again because we came here for specific attention but felt as though I was getting blown off. I was scheduled into routine cardiac rehab sessions, and they were going well. One day I had an echocardiogram scheduled before my cardiac rehab appointment. I thought to myself, "As soon as this is over, I'll go to rehab and then go home to take a shower. I was in that room for a while, and I thought the person performing the ECG was just being thorough, but it turned out, I had a blood clot in my heart for the second time. They immediately admitted me to treat the blood clot and monitor me, so, that day, I never made it to cardiac rehab or back to the house to get that shower. I was placed on blood thinners that consisted of ten days of self-administered shots at home and then medicine in pill form to take until they assessed me again six months later. It was a rollercoaster of events, but I did make it out of the crazy year called 2020. **PRAISE GOD!** What I will say though, is that God is good, and His timing never fails. If I didn't go to that routine appointment to find out that I had a blood clot in my heart, I could've died.

CHAPTER 8

God is with Me

Child Like Faith

Ever since I was a kid, I knew there was something different about me. I could feel it but didn't necessarily know how to describe or even articulate what I was feeling. Trust me. I am not saying that I am special or anything like that because I'm not, and I know that. I guess I was just a little more sensitive to Jesus than most of my peers as I was growing up. I remember quoting Scripture when I was about seven years old or so. The one I remember quoting was ***John 1:1-3*** that read, *"In the beginning was the Word, and the Word was with God, and the Word was God. The same was in the beginning with God. All things were made by him; and without him was not any thing made that was made."*

I got Baptized at the age of eight years old and I remember just feeling so close to God. Oh, how I wish I could have that feeling back in my life. The innocence of a child is to be treasured. I think that's why parents do the best they can to protect their children from the craziness of this world that ends up becoming an inevitable takeover of the child's mind, whether through cartoons, other TV shows, friends, internet, music–I could go on and on.

I used to love to look at the sun peeking its brilliance from behind the clouds and how it creates those rays of light that shine over the land. That was so heavenly to me as a child. Actually, I still love to see it to this day. It really made me feel close to God and would allow me to lose myself in that moment. Being able to feel the presence of God instead of sitting in the reality of what was going on around me. There weren't that many distractions as opposed to the distractions of this era. I felt that God loved me and there was nothing that could get in the way of that.

Then I grew up, and guess what? God still loves me the same, mistakes and all, carelessness and all, but I can't feel that love all the time because now I am set in guilt and shame that makes me feel like I'm so far from God. But nothing could be further from the truth. These distractions can get extremely loud today. God makes room for my mistakes as He teaches me just how much He loves me and just how close He actually is.

Immanuel - God With Us

The Bible says in **Matthew 1:23**, *"BEHOLD, THE VIRGIN SHALL BE WITH CHILD AND SHALL BEAR A SON, AND THEY SHALL CALL HIS NAME IMMANUEL,"* which translated means, *"GOD WITH US."* This is a restating of a passage of Scripture found in Isaiah 7:14 as the Book of Matthew is telling the story of the conception and birth of Jesus. What I want to focus on is the part that says the name Immanuel – God with us. Then if we look at **Psalms 23:4** it says, *"Even though I walk through the valley of the shadow of death, I fear no evil, for You are with me..."* *"You, (God), are with me"* – Immanuel.

The truth is that You've never left. Finding my way through life I wish it could have been easier to keep my mind steady on You, but I gave in to sin a lot. There were times that I wished I could just be perfect because I don't want to sin, I just want to be Christlike. I wonder if most people feel this way but find it impossible to resist temptation as much as they want to. Even the Apostle Paul had to write about this when he said, *"For the good that I want, I do not do, but I practice the very evil that I do not* *want. But if I am doing the very thing I do not want, I am no longer the one doing it, but sin which dwells in me." **Romans 7:19-20**.* The enemy will come in and lie to us all the time to keep us from believing that we are the children of God. He does this because he knows our worth and it makes him sick and jealous.

Hearing the Quiet

When we feel like God is nowhere to be found and that He's not listening or hearing us, this can make us give up on God, but God never gives up on us. It's not Him who doesn't hear us or who is not listening. We're usually the ones not listening or taking the quiet moments to hear from God. A lot of times we get in our own way and block God from our own sight or earshot, (spiritually), but God is with us at all times. When we face the difficult decisions, before we make bad choices, when your father walks out on the family, when you're getting pressured into being careless. Even in times that evil is present God is there.

People ask all the time, "If God is real then why would He allow this or that to happen, and the "this or that," is usually the worst things you can imagine. God does not just simply allow bad things to happen. Evil things happen because of the devil and his evil ways. I feel like God allows things to happen to us for our growth and strength so that in the midst of, or even after the situation God can show you how He was right there with you and kept you through your situation. Later when we find ourselves standing on the other side of the problem, we begin to see our strength as the day comes when we must help someone else who has gone through something similar. When you have endured hardship or trials you start to understand Immanuel is what got you through to the other side.

Faith above Water

It's like when Peter and the disciples went over to the other side of the big lake and the storm arose. They were having a rough time and thought it would be their end. Afterwhile, they see someone like a ghost walking on the water and they were terrified. Jesus tells them not to be afraid because it was Him. Peter challenges the apparition by saying, "Lord if it's you, command me to walk with you on the water." Jesus told him to come out there, and Peter did. Now for a while, Peter was walking on the water toward Jesus, but when he got distracted by his circumstances he started to go under. Jesus wants our faith in Him to be above water not sinking beneath it. We must know that wherever we are and in whatever circumstance, He is right there with us. He wants us to know this because he always keeps His word, and one of His promises to us is that he would never leave nor forsake us. It may not always look like we think it should look, but His promises will remain.

Right when Peter was about to go under, he screamed, "Lord, save me!" immediately, Jesus pulled him up and said to him "You and your little faith. Why did you doubt?" It is important to know what happened next when they climbed back into the boat. The winds died down and the waves calmed, and the rest of the disciples worshiped Him. Why is that important? It is important to know that 1) Sometimes God will put us in situations to test our faith and other times we'll be in situations that He didn't put us in but is fully aware that we are in them. He's watching to see if you're going to realize that He is right there with you and that you have the faith to call on Him and believe that it will all work out in the end. 2) It's also important to know that the God who can calm the wind and the waves can calm any storm that arises in your life. You are not alone because God is with you.

Immanuel.

EPILOGUE

Immanuel in the Valley

Looking back over my life, I can see the thread now. I can see the hand of God moving through every valley, every heartbreak, every miracle, every tear. When I first started writing this book, I thought it would be about the pain that I'd suffered through the years. But as the words came together, I realized it was never just about pain and suffering. It was more than that. It was about presence.

·The presence of God when I lost loved ones.

·The presence of God when my heart literally broke.

·The presence of God when fear whispered louder than faith.

Through every moment, He was there. Even when I couldn't see Him, and even when I didn't want to. I used to think God showed up after the storm to sweep up the broken pieces, but now I know He was there in the storm, holding the pieces together because He holds all things together. I can say with confidence that every valley has purpose. Every scar has a story. Every trial has a truth. The valleys don't define us, they refine us. They strip away what doesn't matter and reveal the God who does. And just when we think it's over, when we've run out of strength, breath, or hope, that's when we feel Immanuel.

Not a distant God that sits on high, but a present God who sits on high even in the valleys. The One who whispers, "I'm still here." Today, as I look at my life, my wife, my children, my family, my faith, I realize that even when bad things happened to me, God was still good working through it all. He carried me when I couldn't stand. He restored me when I was broken. He reminded me that His grace doesn't run out when life gets hard, it runs to us.

So, wherever you are in your journey, no matter what your valley looks like right now, hold on to this truth: God is with you. He always has been. He always will be. And when you look back one day, you'll see that His fingerprints were on every page of your story too.

Reflection & Prayer

Reflection Questions

- Looking back over your own valleys, where do you now see God's fingerprints?
- What lesson or healing has come out of your pain? How can your story be a light for someone else walking through the dark?
- When have you mistaken being "good" for being godly?
- What loss or heartbreak made you question God the most?
- How might God be using your story to heal someone else's

Prayer

Father, thank You for every valley that drew me closer to You. Thank You for being my Shepherd when I was lost, my strength when I was weak, and my peace when my world fell apart. Teach me to live with gratitude for Your presence, to trust Your plan even when I don't understand it, and to share the hope that Immanuel–God with us–still walks with us today. In Jesus' name, Amen.

End Note

The journey doesn't end here. Immanuel still walks with us–in the valleys, in the waiting, in the healing, in the hope. If you don't yet know Him, you can. "For God so loved the world that He gave His only begotten Son, that whoever believes in Him shall not perish, but have everlasting life." John 3:16 God is not distant. He's closer than your next breath. And no matter what life brings–He will always, always be with you.

Acknowledgments

Thank You From the Bottom of My Heart

- First and foremost, I give all glory, honor, and praise to my Lord and Savior, Jesus Christ. Without His grace, this story wouldn't exist. Every word in this book reflects His love, mercy, and presence in my life. I love you, Lord!!

- To my beautiful wife, Jennie — my Beauty, my partner, my answered prayer. You've walked with me through every storm and every sunrise. Thank you for your strength, your patience, and your faith. You've shown me what love anchored in God truly looks like. I love you endlessly!

- To my amazing children — Lala, KJ, Jay, Jo, Juju, and Jesi. You are my greatest blessings. You've given me reasons to fight, to smile, and to keep believing when life tried to break me. I hope this book helps you see that your father's faith was tested and God proved faithful every time. I love you all!

- To my parents — Robert "Turtle" Brown and my late mother, Doretha "Tuffy" Brown — thank you for raising me in love, prayer, and truth. Everything I am today was built on the foundation you gave me. I love you! And to my little sister, Aisha "Nikkii" Beasley, thank you for your love and support through every chapter of life. You've always been one of my biggest cheerleaders. I love you!

- To the Brown - Hungerford Family, Thank you for your love and support through the years. I could not have asked for a better family and support system. I love you!

- To the Stevens Family, I thank you for your support. I love you!
- I want to acknowledge the love and dedication from Rubenia Aldana, (my Mother-In-Law), and Yvonne Brown, (my stepmother). I want you to know that your hard work never goes unnoticed. I love you two!
- To my extended family and friends—those who prayed for me, checked on me, or encouraged me when I couldn't encourage myself—thank you. Your words and love carried me further than you know. Much Love!
- To my church family and every pastor, mentor, and brother or sister in Christ who spoke life over me—I'm grateful for your obedience to God's call. And to every reader holding this book—thank you for walking this journey with me. If even one page brought you closer to God, then every word was worth writing. Through it all, I've learned this: God never wastes a story. He redeems it. He uses it. And He's using mine—right here, right now. God bless you!

Reference Page

Widow Maker, Left Anterior Descending Artery, (LAD). Steven Brown, (May 2020), WebMD article.

All Bible verses are from the New American Standard Bible, (NASB, 1995).

A Personal Invitation

*If this book has touched your heart in any way, I want you to know
— that means the world to me. My prayer in writing Immanuel in
the Valley was never just to tell my story, but to remind you that
God is still writing yours.*

*You are not alone in your valley. God sees you. He's walking with
you. And He's not done with you yet.*

*I'd love to hear how this book has impacted your journey. Your
testimony might be the light someone else needs to find their way
out of the darkness.*

*You can connect with me and share your story by email at
immanuelinthevalley@gmail.com, or through social media
(coming soon). Together, we'll keep spreading the truth that even
in the lowest moments of life, Immanuel — God with us — is still
here.*

Until then, stay encouraged, stay faithful, and keep walking.

The valley is not your ending — it's your beginning.

With love and gratitude,

Keith A. Brown Sr.

About the Author

Keith A. Brown Sr. is a loving husband and devoted father. He is an American author and faith storyteller whose journey through valleys of pain and redemption inspires others to see God's presence in every storm—because the same God who said to the wind and the waves, "Peace, be still," is still calming storms today.

Keith lives in San Antonio, Texas, with his wife, Jennifer, and three of their six children. He became a licensed minister in February 2018 and has been a follower of Jesus Christ since the age of eight.

He has walked through valleys of divorce, legal trials, and serious medical hardship, yet through every low place, he has seen God's hand move. Keith invites readers into his story with the understanding that even when the valley feels lower, God is still present.

Keith A. Brown Sr., author of Immanuel in the Valley: When Bad Things Happen to Good People

immanuelinthevalley@gmail.com

Instagram: @brotha_keith

Notes

Notes

Notes

Notes

www.ingramcontent.com/pod-product-compliance
Lightning Source LLC
Chambersburg PA
CBHW021014160726
47994CB00006B/2513